Discover the Power of TikTok Ads for Your Business in 2023 and Beyond

I0490821

By Hugh Webb

Disclaimer:

The information provided in this book is for educational and informational purposes only. The author is not a licensed professional, and the content should not be considered a substitute for professional advice or services. The reader assumes full responsibility for any actions taken based on the information in this book. The author and publisher are not liable for any damages or negative consequences arising from the use or misuse of the information provided. It is recommended that readers conduct their own research and consult with a professional before making any significant changes to their cleaning routine or use of natural cleaning products.

Table of Contents

Chapter 1: The Evolution of TikTok as a Social Media Platform

TikTok is a social media platform that has quickly become one of the most popular apps in the world. Initially launched in China in 2016 under the name Douyin, it was later introduced to the global market as TikTok in 2017. Since then, TikTok has grown exponentially, becoming the go-to app for millions of users worldwide.

At its core, TikTok is a video-sharing app that allows users to create and share short-form videos with music, sound effects, filters, and other creative elements. These videos can range from dance challenges to comedy skits, lip-syncing to viral songs, and much more.

One of the reasons why TikTok has become so popular is its algorithm that curates content based on user preferences. The app's AI technology analyzes user behavior, such as the videos they like, share, and comment on, to recommend content that matches their interests.

TikTok's success can also be attributed to its accessibility. Anyone with a smartphone can download the app and start creating content. Unlike other social media platforms that require a large following to gain visibility, TikTok provides an equal opportunity for everyone to go viral.

TikTok has also evolved beyond just a social media platform for entertainment. It has become a marketing tool for businesses looking to connect with younger audiences. With its massive user base, TikTok offers brands a unique opportunity to reach a wide audience in a short amount of time.

Another significant factor in TikTok's evolution is its global expansion. The app has been able to penetrate new markets worldwide, with a particularly strong presence in India, the United States, and Brazil.

As TikTok continues to grow, it will likely continue to evolve to meet the changing needs of its users. The app has already introduced new features, such as live streaming and e-commerce integrations, to keep up with the latest trends and stay ahead of the competition.

In conclusion, TikTok has come a long way since its launch in 2016. With its unique algorithm, accessibility, and global expansion, TikTok has become a social media giant and a game-changer in the advertising world. As the platform continues to evolve, businesses and users alike can expect even more exciting changes in the years to come.

Chapter 2: The Importance of Advertising on TikTok

TikTok has quickly become one of the most popular social media platforms worldwide, with over 1 billion active users. As such, it has become an essential platform for businesses looking to reach younger audiences and increase brand awareness. Here are some reasons why advertising on TikTok is so important:

1. Large and Engaged User Base: TikTok's massive user base is a significant reason for businesses to advertise on the platform. With over 1 billion active users, TikTok provides brands with a vast audience to showcase their products or services. Furthermore, TikTok users are highly engaged, with an average session time of 52 minutes per day, making it a prime platform for brand exposure.

2. Opportunities for Viral Content: TikTok's algorithm can help brands go viral quickly. With a well-planned advertising campaign, brands can create videos that appeal to the algorithm and reach millions of users. The platform's algorithm prioritizes content that is engaging, unique, and trending, which provides an excellent opportunity for brands to create viral content.

3. Targeting Capabilities: TikTok has advanced targeting capabilities that allow businesses to reach their target audience. Advertisers can target users based on demographics, location, interests, behaviors, and more. These targeting capabilities enable brands to reach users who are most likely to engage with their content, resulting in more effective advertising campaigns.

4. Diverse Ad Formats: TikTok offers several ad formats that provide businesses with a range of options to showcase their brand. These include In-Feed Ads, Brand Takeovers, Hashtag Challenges, Branded Effects, and more. Each ad format has its strengths and can be used to achieve different advertising objectives, such as increasing brand awareness, driving sales, or promoting a new product.
5. Cost-Effective Advertising: Advertising on TikTok can be more cost-effective compared to other social media platforms. TikTok's advertising platform offers competitive pricing, making it an affordable option for businesses of all sizes. Furthermore, the platform's targeting capabilities and engaging content can help businesses maximize their return on investment (ROI).

In conclusion, advertising on TikTok is essential for businesses looking to reach younger audiences and increase brand awareness. With a large and engaged user base, opportunities for viral content, advanced targeting capabilities, diverse ad formats, and cost-effective pricing, TikTok provides businesses with a unique opportunity to connect with their target audience and achieve their advertising goals.

Chapter 3: Why TikTok Ads are Becoming More Popular Among Businesses

TikTok has become a massive phenomenon worldwide, and its popularity shows no signs of slowing down. As such, businesses are starting to take notice and are increasingly using TikTok ads as a part of their marketing strategy. Here are some reasons why TikTok ads are becoming more popular among businesses:

1. Reach a Younger Audience: TikTok has a younger user base than other social media platforms, making it an ideal platform for businesses targeting the Gen Z and Millennial demographics. This younger audience is tech-savvy, more likely to engage with branded content, and can be challenging to reach on other platforms.
2. Creative Opportunities: TikTok's video-based platform allows businesses to get creative with their ads. TikTok ads are designed to blend seamlessly with organic content, and there are various ad formats to choose from, such as In-Feed Ads, Hashtag Challenges, and Branded Effects. These formats provide businesses with an opportunity to showcase their products or services in a unique and engaging way.
3. Viral Potential: TikTok's algorithm prioritizes content that is engaging, unique, and trending, making it possible for TikTok ads to go viral. A well-executed TikTok ad campaign can generate significant reach and engagement in a short amount of time, leading to increased brand awareness and potentially even sales.

4. Targeting Capabilities: TikTok's advanced targeting capabilities allow businesses to reach their target audience effectively. Advertisers can target users based on demographics, interests, behaviors, and more. These targeting capabilities enable businesses to deliver their ads to the users who are most likely to engage with their content.

5. Competitive Pricing: Advertising on TikTok can be more cost-effective compared to other social media platforms. TikTok's advertising platform offers competitive pricing, making it an affordable option for businesses of all sizes. Furthermore, the platform's targeting capabilities and engaging content can help businesses maximize their return on investment (ROI).

In conclusion, TikTok ads are becoming increasingly popular among businesses for several reasons. TikTok's large and engaged user base, creative opportunities, viral potential, targeting capabilities, and competitive pricing make it an attractive option for businesses looking to reach younger audiences and increase brand awareness. As TikTok continues to evolve and expand, businesses can expect even more exciting opportunities for advertising on the platform in the future.

Chapter 4: The Different Types of TikTok Ads

TikTok offers various ad formats that businesses can use to showcase their products or services. Each ad format has its strengths and can be used to achieve different advertising objectives. Here are the different types of TikTok ads:

1. In-Feed Ads: In-Feed Ads are full-screen ads that appear in users' "For You" page feed. These ads are similar to native TikTok videos and can be up to 60 seconds long. In-Feed Ads can include clickable links to the business's website or app, making them an excellent option for driving website traffic and increasing brand awareness.
2. Brand Takeovers: Brand Takeovers are full-screen ads that appear as soon as a user opens the TikTok app. These ads can be images or videos and can include a clickable link to the business's website or app. Brand Takeovers are an effective way to grab users' attention and increase brand awareness.
3. Hashtag Challenges: Hashtag Challenges are a popular ad format on TikTok that encourages users to create and share content using a specific hashtag. Hashtag Challenges can be sponsored by a business and can include a call-to-action for users to visit the business's website or app. Hashtag Challenges are an excellent option for increasing user-generated content and brand engagement.
4. Branded Effects: Branded Effects are augmented reality filters that businesses can create to promote their products or services. These filters can be used by TikTok users in their videos and can include a clickable link to the business's website or app. Branded Effects are a unique way to increase brand awareness and engage with users on a more personal level.

5. TopView Ads: TopView Ads are full-screen video ads that appear immediately after a user opens the TikTok app. These ads can be up to 60 seconds long and can include a clickable link to the business's website or app. TopView Ads are an excellent option for businesses looking to make a strong first impression and increase brand awareness.
6. Branded Hashtag Challenges: Branded Hashtag Challenges are a combination of the Hashtag Challenges and Branded Effects ad formats. These challenges feature a sponsored hashtag and a branded augmented reality filter, encouraging users to create and share content using both. Branded Hashtag Challenges are an effective way to increase user-generated content and brand engagement.

In conclusion, TikTok offers various ad formats that businesses can use to reach their target audience and achieve their advertising objectives. In-Feed Ads, Brand Takeovers, Hashtag Challenges, Branded Effects, TopView Ads, and Branded Hashtag Challenges all provide unique opportunities for businesses to showcase their products or services and increase brand awareness. By selecting the right ad format for their advertising objectives, businesses can create engaging and effective TikTok ad campaigns.

Chapter 5: How to Create a TikTok Ad Campaign

Creating a successful TikTok Ad campaign requires careful planning and execution. Here are the steps to create a TikTok Ad campaign:

1. Set Advertising Objectives: The first step in creating a TikTok Ad campaign is to identify your advertising objectives. Do you want to increase brand awareness, drive website traffic, or increase sales? Your objectives will dictate the type of ad format you choose and the targeting options you select.
2. Choose Ad Format: Based on your advertising objectives, select the most suitable ad format. In-Feed Ads, Brand Takeovers, Hashtag Challenges, Branded Effects, TopView Ads, and Branded Hashtag Challenges are the different types of ad formats available on TikTok.
3. Define Target Audience: Once you have chosen the ad format, define your target audience. TikTok offers various targeting options, including age, gender, interests, location, and device type. Narrowing down your target audience will ensure that your ad is shown to the right people.
4. Set Budget: Set your ad campaign budget, taking into account the ad format, targeting options, and duration of the campaign. TikTok offers different bidding options, including cost per click (CPC) and cost per impression (CPM).
5. Create Ad Content: The next step is to create ad content that is engaging, attention-grabbing, and aligns with your advertising objectives. Use high-quality visuals and a clear call-to-action to encourage users to interact with your ad.

6. Monitor Ad Performance: Once your ad campaign is live, monitor its performance regularly. TikTok provides detailed analytics that can help you understand how your ad is performing, including impressions, clicks, and engagement. Use this information to optimize your ad campaign and improve its performance.
7. Test and Experiment: Don't be afraid to test and experiment with different ad formats, targeting options, and ad content. Analyze the results and make adjustments to improve the performance of your ad campaign.

In conclusion, creating a successful TikTok Ad campaign requires careful planning and execution. By setting clear advertising objectives, choosing the right ad format, defining your target audience, setting a budget, creating engaging ad content, monitoring ad performance, and testing and experimenting, businesses can create effective TikTok Ad campaigns that achieve their advertising objectives.

Chapter 6: Tips for Optimizing Your TikTok Ads

Optimizing your TikTok Ads is crucial to ensure that your ads reach the right audience and achieve your advertising objectives. Here are some tips for optimizing your TikTok Ads:

1. Choose the Right Ad Format: Choosing the right ad format is critical to the success of your ad campaign. Evaluate your advertising objectives and choose the ad format that aligns with them.
2. Define Your Target Audience: Defining your target audience is essential to ensure that your ads are shown to the right people. Use TikTok's targeting options to narrow down your audience and make your ads more effective.
3. Create Engaging Ad Content: Engaging ad content is key to grabbing users' attention and encouraging them to interact with your ad. Use high-quality visuals, clear messaging, and a strong call-to-action to make your ad stand out.
4. Test Different Ad Content: Testing different ad content can help you identify what works and what doesn't. Experiment with different visuals, messaging, and calls-to-action to find the optimal ad content for your target audience.
5. Optimize Bidding Strategies: TikTok offers different bidding strategies, including cost-per-click (CPC) and cost-per-impression (CPM). Experiment with different bidding strategies to find the most cost-effective option for your ad campaign.
6. Monitor Ad Performance: Regularly monitor your ad performance to identify areas of improvement. Use TikTok's analytics to measure impressions, clicks, and engagement rates and adjust your ad campaign accordingly.

7. A/B Test Your Ad Campaign: A/B testing can help you identify which elements of your ad campaign are most effective. Test different ad formats, targeting options, ad content, and bidding strategies to optimize your ad campaign's performance.
8. Keep Up with Trends: TikTok is a dynamic platform that evolves rapidly. Stay up-to-date with the latest trends and incorporate them into your ad campaign to make it more relevant and appealing to users.

By following these tips, businesses can optimize their TikTok Ad campaigns and achieve their advertising objectives. TikTok is a powerful platform that offers a unique opportunity to reach a vast and engaged audience. By creating engaging ad content, targeting the right audience, and optimizing ad performance, businesses can create effective TikTok Ad campaigns that drive results.

Chapter 7: The Latest Trends in TikTok Ads

TikTok is a dynamic platform that constantly evolves, and advertising on TikTok has become increasingly popular among businesses. Here are some of the latest trends in TikTok Ads:

1. Influencer Marketing: Influencer marketing has become a popular trend in TikTok Ads. Brands partner with popular influencers on the platform to create sponsored content that promotes their products or services.
2. User-Generated Content: User-generated content is another trend in TikTok Ads. Brands encourage users to create content using their products or services and share it on the platform, creating a buzz and increasing brand awareness.
3. Live Streaming: Live streaming is becoming more prevalent on TikTok, and brands are taking advantage of this trend by hosting live events, such as product launches or Q&A sessions, to engage with their audience.
4. Interactive Ads: Interactive ads, such as Hashtag Challenges and Branded Effects, are becoming increasingly popular on TikTok. These ad formats encourage users to interact with the brand and its products, increasing engagement and brand awareness.
5. Personalization: Personalization is a growing trend in TikTok Ads. Brands are creating personalized ads that target users based on their interests, behaviors, and preferences, making the ad experience more relevant and engaging.
6. Short-Form Video Ads: Short-form video ads are a popular trend on TikTok. Brands are creating short, attention-grabbing ads that resonate with users and communicate their message effectively.

7. E-commerce Integration: E-commerce integration is a trend that allows users to make purchases directly on the platform. Brands are leveraging this trend by creating shoppable ads that enable users to purchase products with just a few clicks.

By staying up-to-date with the latest trends in TikTok Ads, businesses can create more effective ad campaigns that resonate with their audience and achieve their advertising objectives. TikTok is a dynamic platform that offers a unique opportunity for brands to connect with a vast and engaged audience. By incorporating the latest trends into their ad campaigns, businesses can maximize their reach and impact on the platform.

Chapter 8: How to Stay Up-to-Date with TikTok Ad Trends

Staying up-to-date with the latest trends in TikTok Ads is essential for businesses to create effective ad campaigns that resonate with their target audience. Here are some ways to stay informed about the latest TikTok Ad trends:

1. Follow TikTok's Official Channels: Follow TikTok's official channels, including their blog and social media accounts, to stay informed about the latest platform updates, features, and trends.
2. Attend Industry Events: Attend industry events, such as marketing conferences and webinars, to learn about the latest trends and best practices in TikTok Ads.
3. Network with Other Professionals: Network with other marketing professionals, especially those who are active on TikTok. Share insights and tips with each other to stay informed about the latest trends in the platform.
4. Use TikTok's Advertising Resources: TikTok provides a range of resources to help businesses create effective ad campaigns. Use these resources, including their ad guidelines and creative toolkit, to stay informed about the latest ad formats and trends.
5. Monitor Competitors: Monitor your competitors' TikTok Ads to stay informed about their ad strategies and creative approaches. This can help you identify new trends and best practices in TikTok Ads.
6. Analyze Your Ad Performance: Analyze your ad performance regularly to identify areas of improvement and adjust your ad campaign accordingly. This can help you stay up-to-date with the latest trends in TikTok Ads and optimize your ad campaign's performance.

7. Keep an Eye on Popular Content: Keep an eye on popular content on TikTok to identify new trends and creative approaches that resonate with users. This can help you create more engaging ad content and stay ahead of the curve.

By staying up-to-date with the latest TikTok Ad trends, businesses can create more effective ad campaigns that resonate with their audience and achieve their advertising objectives. TikTok is a dynamic platform that evolves rapidly, and staying informed about the latest trends is critical to maximizing your impact on the platform.

Chapter 9: How to Incorporate Trends into Your TikTok Ad Campaigns

Incorporating the latest trends into your TikTok Ad campaigns can help your brand stay relevant and engage with your target audience. Here are some tips on how to incorporate trends into your TikTok Ad campaigns:

1. Stay Up-to-Date: Stay up-to-date with the latest trends in TikTok Ads by following the latest news, attending industry events, and monitoring your competitors.
2. Identify Relevant Trends: Identify trends that are relevant to your brand and align with your advertising objectives. For example, if you're promoting a new product, consider using a Hashtag Challenge to generate buzz and encourage user-generated content.
3. Create Engaging Content: Create engaging content that resonates with your audience and incorporates the latest trends. For example, if the latest trend is a dance challenge, consider creating a branded dance challenge that promotes your product or service.
4. Partner with Influencers: Partner with influencers who are active in your industry and have a large following on TikTok. They can help you leverage the latest trends and create sponsored content that promotes your brand and products.
5. Use Branded Effects: Branded Effects are a popular trend in TikTok Ads and can help your brand create engaging content that resonates with your audience. Consider creating a Branded Effect that aligns with your brand and advertising objectives.
6. Test and Optimize: Test different ad formats and content to see what resonates with your audience and achieves your advertising objectives. Use data and insights to optimize your ad campaign and stay ahead of the curve.

7. Be Authentic: While it's important to incorporate the latest trends into your TikTok Ad campaigns, it's also important to be authentic and stay true to your brand. Ensure that your ad content aligns with your brand's voice and values to maintain brand authenticity and credibility.

By incorporating the latest trends into your TikTok Ad campaigns, businesses can create more engaging and effective ad content that resonates with their target audience. TikTok is a dynamic platform that offers unique opportunities for brands to connect with a vast and engaged audience. By leveraging the latest trends and best practices, businesses can maximize their impact on the platform and achieve their advertising objectives.

Chapter 10: Case Studies of Successful TikTok Ad Campaigns

To truly understand the potential of TikTok Ads and how to make the most of the platform, it's important to look at some successful case studies. Here are a few examples of successful TikTok Ad campaigns:

1. Gymshark's Hashtag Challenge: UK-based fitness apparel brand Gymshark launched a Hashtag Challenge on TikTok called #gymshark66, encouraging users to share their fitness journey for 66 days. The challenge was a huge success, generating over 17,000 user-generated videos and over 200 million views. As a result, Gymshark saw a significant increase in brand awareness and engagement.

2. Fenty Beauty's Branded Hashtag Challenge: Fenty Beauty, the cosmetics brand owned by Rihanna, launched a Branded Hashtag Challenge on TikTok called #FentyBeautyHouseParty, encouraging users to create their own makeup looks using Fenty Beauty products. The challenge generated over 4.8 billion views and helped Fenty Beauty reach a younger, more diverse audience.

3. Too Faced Cosmetics' Influencer Partnership: Too Faced Cosmetics partnered with popular TikTok influencer Avani Gregg to promote their new mascara. Avani created a series of sponsored videos showcasing the mascara, which generated over 11 million views and helped Too Faced Cosmetics increase brand awareness and product sales.

4. Ocean Spray's TikTok Moment: Ocean Spray, the cranberry juice brand, had a viral moment on TikTok when a video featuring a man riding a skateboard and drinking Ocean Spray juice while listening to Fleetwood Mac's "Dreams" went viral. The video generated millions of views and inspired countless user-generated videos, resulting in a significant increase in brand awareness and product sales.

These case studies demonstrate the power of TikTok Ads and how businesses can leverage the platform to achieve their advertising objectives. By creating engaging and authentic content, partnering with influencers, and leveraging the latest trends and ad formats, businesses can maximize their impact on the platform and reach a vast and engaged audience.

Chapter 11: Lessons Learned from Successful TikTok Ad Campaigns

After reviewing successful TikTok ad campaigns, it's important to take note of the lessons learned. Here are some key takeaways:

1. Authenticity is key: TikTok users value authenticity and are more likely to engage with content that feels genuine and relatable. Successful campaigns often feature user-generated content or partner with influencers who have a strong connection with their audience.
2. Engage with the community: TikTok is a highly social platform, and successful campaigns often involve user participation or engagement. Hashtag challenges and interactive ads can help create a sense of community and foster engagement.
3. Stay on top of trends: TikTok is known for its fast-paced trends, and successful campaigns often incorporate the latest memes, music, and video formats. Brands that are able to keep up with the latest trends are more likely to resonate with the platform's young and diverse audience.
4. Leverage influencers: TikTok has a thriving influencer community, and partnering with popular creators can help increase brand awareness and drive engagement. Influencers can provide a personal touch to campaigns and help brands reach niche audiences.
5. Measure success: As with any advertising campaign, it's important to track and measure success. Brands should set clear objectives and use data analytics to evaluate performance and optimize their campaigns.

By taking these lessons into account, businesses can create effective TikTok ad campaigns that resonate with the platform's unique audience and drive meaningful results.

Chapter 12: Applying Lessons Learned to Your Own TikTok Ad Campaigns

Now that we've reviewed the lessons learned from successful TikTok ad campaigns, it's time to apply these lessons to your own campaigns. Here are some tips on how to incorporate these lessons into your TikTok ad strategy:

1. Be authentic: When creating TikTok Ads, focus on creating authentic content that resonates with your target audience. Use real people and user-generated content when possible to make your ads more relatable.
2. Engage with the community: To drive engagement, create ads that encourage user participation. Consider using hashtag challenges or interactive ads that ask users to take action.
3. Stay on top of trends: Keep a close eye on the latest TikTok trends, and try to incorporate them into your ads whenever possible. Don't be afraid to experiment with new formats or styles of content to keep your ads fresh and engaging.
4. Leverage influencers: Consider partnering with influencers who have a strong following on TikTok. Look for creators who align with your brand values and can help you reach a niche audience.
5. Measure success: Set clear objectives for your campaigns and use data analytics to measure performance. Use this data to optimize your campaigns and make adjustments as needed.

By applying these lessons to your TikTok ad campaigns, you can increase the chances of success on the platform. Remember to stay true to your brand values and create content that resonates with your target audience. With the right strategy and execution, TikTok Ads can be a powerful tool for driving brand awareness, engagement, and conversions.

Chapter 13: Predictions for the Future of TikTok Ads

As TikTok continues to grow and evolve, what does the future hold for TikTok Ads? Here are some predictions for the future of advertising on TikTok:

1. Increased competition: As more brands realize the potential of TikTok Ads, the competition for ad space will increase. This means that brands will need to be more creative and innovative with their ad campaigns to stand out from the crowd.
2. More advanced targeting options: TikTok is likely to continue to improve its targeting capabilities, allowing brands to reach more specific audiences. This could include more sophisticated demographic targeting or even targeting based on user behavior.
3. Integration with e-commerce: TikTok has already begun testing e-commerce features, and it's likely that the platform will continue to integrate with e-commerce in the future. This could include shoppable ads or even a dedicated TikTok shopping section.
4. Greater use of augmented reality (AR): TikTok has already shown a strong interest in AR, with features like its AR Branded Effects. It's likely that we'll see more brands incorporating AR into their TikTok ad campaigns in the future.
5. Continued growth: TikTok's user base is expected to continue to grow, particularly among older age groups. This means that TikTok Ads will become an increasingly important advertising channel for brands looking to reach a diverse and engaged audience.

Overall, the future of TikTok Ads looks bright, with continued growth and innovation on the horizon. Brands that stay ahead of the curve and are willing to experiment with new ad formats and strategies will be well-positioned to succeed on the platform.

Chapter 14: How TikTok Ads Will Continue to Evolve

As TikTok Ads continue to grow in popularity, the platform is likely to continue to evolve to meet the needs of both advertisers and users. Here are some ways in which TikTok Ads may evolve in the future:

1. More interactive ad formats: TikTok is known for its engaging and interactive content, and we can expect to see more interactive ad formats in the future. This could include gamified ads or ads that allow users to interact with a brand's products or services.
2. Increased personalization: As TikTok's targeting capabilities improve, we can expect to see more personalized ad experiences for users. This could include ads that are tailored to a user's interests, location, or previous behavior on the platform.
3. Integration with other platforms: TikTok has already begun to integrate with other platforms, such as Shopify, to allow for seamless e-commerce experiences. In the future, we could see even more integration with other platforms and technologies, such as virtual and augmented reality.
4. Enhanced measurement and analytics: As TikTok Ads become more important for brands, we can expect to see more advanced measurement and analytics capabilities. This will allow brands to better track the performance of their ad campaigns and make data-driven decisions.
5. Emphasis on brand safety and transparency: As with any advertising platform, brand safety and transparency are important considerations for advertisers. TikTok is likely to continue to improve its brand safety measures and provide more transparency around ad placement and performance.

Overall, the future of TikTok Ads looks bright, with continued innovation and improvements on the horizon. Advertisers who stay up-to-date with the latest trends and technology will be well-positioned to succeed on the platform and reach TikTok's growing audience.

Chapter 15: How Businesses Can Prepare for the Future of TikTok Ads

As TikTok Ads continue to evolve, businesses need to stay ahead of the curve to maximize their success on the platform.

Here are some tips for preparing for the future of TikTok Ads:

1. Keep an eye on emerging trends: Stay up-to-date with the latest trends and technologies on TikTok, and be prepared to adapt your ad strategy accordingly. This may mean experimenting with new ad formats, targeting capabilities, or measurement and analytics tools.

2. Invest in high-quality creative: TikTok is a visually-driven platform, and high-quality creative is essential for standing out in users' feeds. Invest in eye-catching videos that capture the attention of your target audience and align with your brand's message and values.

3. Focus on engagement: As TikTok Ads become more interactive and personalized, engagement will become even more important for success on the platform. Aim to create ads that encourage users to engage with your brand, whether that's by commenting, liking, or sharing your content.

4. Prioritize brand safety and transparency: With the rise of social media scrutiny and ad fraud, it's more important than ever to prioritize brand safety and transparency. Make sure your ad campaigns align with your brand's values and are placed in safe and appropriate contexts.

5. Partner with experts: TikTok Ads can be complex, and it's important to have the right expertise and support in place to maximize your success on the platform. Consider partnering with a TikTok Ads agency or working with a consultant who has experience with the platform.

By following these tips, businesses can prepare for the future of TikTok Ads and position themselves for success on this rapidly-evolving platform. As TikTok continues to grow and innovate, it's essential to stay ahead of the curve and embrace new opportunities for reaching and engaging with your target audience.

Chapter 16: A List of Resources for Creating and Optimizing TikTok Ads

Creating and optimizing TikTok Ads can be a complex and ever-evolving process, but there are a number of resources available to help businesses navigate the platform and maximize their success. Here are some of the top resources for creating and optimizing TikTok Ads:

1. TikTok Ads Help Center: The TikTok Ads Help Center provides a wealth of information on creating and optimizing ads on the platform. From setting up your account to launching your first campaign, the Help Center offers step-by-step guidance and best practices for success.
2. TikTok Ads Manager: The TikTok Ads Manager is the platform's ad management tool, which allows businesses to create, manage, and optimize their ad campaigns. The Ads Manager provides a range of targeting and optimization options, as well as detailed reporting and analytics.
3. TikTok Ads Academy: The TikTok Ads Academy is a comprehensive learning platform that offers a range of courses and resources on advertising on the platform. From beginner-level courses to advanced optimization strategies, the Ads Academy is a valuable resource for businesses looking to improve their TikTok Ads performance.
4. TikTok Creator Fund: The TikTok Creator Fund is a program that provides financial support to content creators on the platform. By partnering with creators, businesses can tap into their audiences and create engaging and authentic content that resonates with their target audience.

5. TikTok Marketing Partners: TikTok Marketing Partners are third-party vendors and agencies that have been vetted and approved by TikTok for their expertise in advertising on the platform. By working with a Marketing Partner, businesses can access advanced tools and services for optimizing their TikTok Ads campaigns.

By leveraging these resources and staying up-to-date with the latest trends and best practices, businesses can create and optimize high-performing TikTok Ads campaigns that reach and engage their target audience. Whether you're a seasoned marketer or new to the platform, there's never been a better time to invest in TikTok Ads and take your business to the next level.

Chapter 17: Tips for Finding the Right TikTok Ads Agency or Consultant

Creating and optimizing TikTok Ads can be a challenging process, especially for businesses that are new to the platform. One way to overcome this challenge is to work with a TikTok Ads agency or consultant who can provide expert guidance and support. However, not all agencies and consultants are created equal, and it's important to choose the right partner to ensure the success of your campaigns. Here are some tips for finding the right TikTok Ads agency or consultant for your business:

1. Look for expertise: When evaluating potential TikTok Ads partners, look for those who have demonstrated expertise in the platform and a track record of success. Ask for case studies or examples of successful campaigns they have run, and look for reviews or testimonials from previous clients.
2. Evaluate their approach: The best TikTok Ads partners will take a strategic approach to your campaigns, considering factors such as your target audience, goals, and budget. Avoid partners who offer a one-size-fits-all approach or make unrealistic promises about results.
3. Assess their communication and responsiveness: Good communication is key to a successful partnership. Look for partners who are responsive and proactive in their communication, and who provide regular updates and reporting on your campaigns.
4. Consider their pricing model: TikTok Ads agencies and consultants may offer a range of pricing models, including flat fees, hourly rates, or performance-based pricing. Choose a partner whose pricing model aligns with your budget and goals, and who is transparent about their fees and billing practices.

5. Check their credentials: Finally, it's important to ensure that any TikTok Ads agency or consultant you work with is licensed and accredited, and adheres to industry best practices and ethical standards.

By taking the time to research and evaluate potential TikTok Ads partners, businesses can find a partner who can provide the expertise, support, and guidance needed to create and optimize high-performing campaigns on the platform. With the right partner by your side, you can leverage the full potential of TikTok Ads and take your business to the next level.

Chapter 18: How to Measure the Success of Your TikTok Ad Campaigns

Measuring the success of your TikTok Ad campaigns is essential to understanding the impact of your marketing efforts and making data-driven decisions for future campaigns. Here are some key metrics to track and methods for measuring the success of your TikTok Ads:

1. Impressions: The number of times your ad was displayed to TikTok users.
2. Click-through rate (CTR): The percentage of users who clicked on your ad after seeing it.
3. Engagement rate: The percentage of users who engaged with your ad (such as liking or commenting) relative to the number of impressions.
4. Conversions: The number of users who took a desired action, such as making a purchase or signing up for a newsletter, after seeing your ad.
5. Return on investment (ROI): The ratio of revenue generated to the cost of the ad campaign.

To track these metrics, TikTok provides a robust analytics dashboard that allows you to monitor the performance of your campaigns in real-time. In addition to this, you can also use third-party analytics tools to gain deeper insights into the performance of your campaigns and track additional metrics that are important to your business.

When measuring the success of your TikTok Ad campaigns, it's important to establish clear goals and benchmarks for success. This will allow you to determine whether your campaigns are meeting your expectations and adjust your strategy accordingly. Additionally, it's important to measure the success of your campaigns over time, rather than just on a campaign-by-campaign basis, to identify trends and patterns in your marketing performance.

By measuring the success of your TikTok Ad campaigns and using the insights gained to optimize your marketing strategy, you can continue to improve the effectiveness of your campaigns and drive real results for your business.

Chapter 19: Summary of Key Takeaways from the Book

In this book, we have explored the evolution of TikTok as a social media platform and the importance of advertising on this platform. We have discussed the different types of TikTok Ads and how to create a successful ad campaign, as well as tips for optimizing your ads and staying up-to-date with the latest trends.
We have also examined case studies of successful TikTok Ad campaigns and the lessons learned from these campaigns, along with how to apply these lessons to your own campaigns. Additionally, we have looked at predictions for the future of TikTok Ads and how businesses can prepare for these changes.

Here are the key takeaways from this book:

1. TikTok is a rapidly growing social media platform that offers unique opportunities for businesses to reach a younger demographic.
2. Advertising on TikTok can be an effective way to increase brand awareness, engagement, and conversions.
3. There are several types of TikTok Ads, including in-feed ads, brand takeovers, and sponsored hashtag challenges, each with its own strengths and weaknesses.
4. When creating a TikTok Ad campaign, it is important to establish clear goals, target the right audience, and create engaging content that resonates with your audience.
5. Staying up-to-date with the latest trends in TikTok Ads is crucial to keeping your campaigns fresh and relevant.

6. By examining case studies of successful TikTok Ad campaigns, businesses can learn valuable lessons about what works and what doesn't in this space.
7. To measure the success of your TikTok Ad campaigns, it is important to track metrics such as impressions, click-through rate, engagement rate, conversions, and return on investment.
8. Finally, businesses should be prepared for the future of TikTok Ads, which will likely include new ad formats, targeting options, and creative tools.

By applying these key takeaways to your own TikTok Ad campaigns, you can improve the effectiveness of your marketing efforts and drive real results for your business.

Chapter 20: Glossary of TikTok Ads Terminology

If you're new to advertising on TikTok, you may come across some terminology that you're unfamiliar with. To help you navigate the world of TikTok Ads, here are some key terms to know:

1. In-feed ads: These are ads that appear in a user's TikTok feed, similar to a regular TikTok video.
2. Brand takeover: This is an ad format that takes over the user's screen when they first open the TikTok app.
3. Sponsored hashtag challenge: This is an ad format that encourages users to create and share content using a branded hashtag.
4. Top View: This is a type of brand takeover ad that plays as soon as the user opens the app and is in full-screen format.
5. Branded effects: These are augmented reality (AR) filters and effects that can be used in TikTok videos and are branded with a company's logo or message.
6. Click-through rate (CTR): This is the percentage of people who clicked on your ad after seeing it.
7. Cost per click (CPC): This is the amount you pay each time someone clicks on your ad.
8. Cost per impression (CPM): This is the amount you pay for every 1,000 times your ad is shown.
9. Engagement rate: This is the percentage of people who engaged with your ad, such as by liking, commenting, or sharing it.
10. Retargeting: This is the practice of showing ads to people who have already interacted with your brand, such as by visiting your website or following you on social media.
11. Lookalike audience: This is a targeting option that allows you to reach people who are similar to your existing customers or followers.

12. Conversion rate: This is the percentage of people who completed a desired action, such as making a purchase or filling out a form, after clicking on your ad.

By understanding these key terms and how they apply to TikTok Ads, you can better optimize your campaigns and achieve your marketing goals.

Chapter 21: TikTok Ads Campaign Checklist

Creating a successful TikTok Ads campaign requires careful planning and execution. To help you stay organized and make sure you don't miss any important steps, here's a checklist you can use for your next TikTok Ads campaign:

1. Define your goals: Before you start creating your ad, decide what you want to achieve with your campaign. Do you want to drive sales, increase brand awareness, or encourage user engagement? Defining your goals will help you create a more effective ad.
2. Know your target audience: Who do you want to reach with your ad? Define your target audience based on factors such as age, gender, location, interests, and behavior.
3. Choose your ad format: There are several ad formats available on TikTok, including in-feed ads, brand takeover, sponsored hashtag challenge, and branded effects. Choose the format that best suits your goals and target audience.
4. Create your ad: Use high-quality visuals, clear messaging, and a strong call-to-action to create an effective ad. Be sure to follow TikTok's ad guidelines and use the correct ad specs for your chosen format.
5. Set your budget and bid strategy: Decide how much you want to spend on your campaign and choose a bidding strategy that aligns with your goals.
6. Choose your targeting options: Use TikTok's targeting options to reach your desired audience, such as by location, interests, behavior, and lookalike audiences.
7. Monitor and optimize your campaign: Keep an eye on your campaign's performance and adjust your targeting, budget, and ad creatives as needed to improve results.

8. Measure your success: Use metrics such as click-through rate, engagement rate, and conversion rate to track your campaign's success and make data-driven decisions for future campaigns.

By following this checklist, you can create a successful TikTok Ads campaign that reaches your desired audience and achieves your marketing goals.

Chapter 22: Sample TikTok Ads Creative Brief

A creative brief is an important document that outlines the key elements of your TikTok Ads campaign, including your goals, target audience, messaging, and more. Here is a sample TikTok Ads creative brief to help you get started.

1. Background Information

Provide some background information on your company, product or service, and the purpose of the TikTok Ads campaign. This could include details such as:
- Company name and industry
- Product or service being promoted
- Current marketing strategy and advertising efforts
- Objective of the TikTok Ads campaign

2. Target Audience

Identify your target audience for the TikTok Ads campaign. This should include details such as:
- Age range
- Gender
- Location
- Interests
- Behavior on the platform

3. Key Message

Outline the key message you want to convey to your target audience through your TikTok Ads campaign. This could be a product feature, promotion, or brand message.

4. Creative Concept

Describe the creative concept for the TikTok Ads campaign. This should include details such as:
- The tone and style of the video(s)
- The visual elements (colors, imagery, etc.)

- The type of music or sound effects used
- Any special effects or animations
- The overall feel and vibe of the ad

5. Call-to-Action (CTA)

Include a clear and specific call-to-action (CTA) in your TikTok Ads campaign. This could be something like "Shop Now" or "Learn More."

6. Budget

Outline the budget for the TikTok Ads campaign. This should include details such as:
- Total budget for the campaign
- Amount allocated for each individual ad
- Any additional costs, such as production expenses

7. Timeline

Provide a timeline for the TikTok Ads campaign, including key milestones and deadlines.

8. Metrics and Reporting

Outline the metrics you will use to measure the success of the TikTok Ads campaign, and how you will report on these metrics. This could include details such as:
- Views and impressions
- Click-through rates (CTR)
- Conversion rates
- Cost per click (CPC) or cost per impression (CPM)
- Any other relevant KPIs

By using a creative brief for your TikTok Ads campaign, you can ensure that all stakeholders are aligned on the key elements of the campaign and that it is optimized for success.

Epilogue:

As we approach the end of 2023, it's clear that TikTok Ads have become an integral part of the digital marketing landscape. Businesses of all sizes have recognized the power of the platform in reaching their target audience and increasing their brand awareness.

In the year since the release of TikTok Ads 2023 and Beyond, we've seen countless success stories from businesses that have implemented the strategies outlined in the book. From small startups to major corporations, TikTok Ads have helped businesses across industries to stand out from the competition and drive business growth.

But the world of digital marketing never stands still, and neither does TikTok. As the platform continues to evolve, so too do the strategies and best practices for advertising on it. It's important for businesses to stay up to date on the latest trends and updates in order to remain competitive in the marketplace.

That's why the insights and guidance provided in TikTok Ads 2023 and Beyond remain as valuable as ever. Whether you're a seasoned marketer or just starting out in the world of digital advertising, this book is your go-to resource for all things TikTok Ads.

So as we look ahead to the future, let's continue to harness the power of TikTok Ads to drive business success and stay ahead of the curve in the fast-paced world of digital marketing.